Desire,

Thanks so much for [...]
I trust this book will bring you great value in 2023 and beyond.

God bless,
Joe Escobar

WINNING THE DAY

WINNING THE DAY

An Entrepreneur's Guide
to
Morning and Evening Routine Mastery

Jose Escobar

Copyright © 2023 Jose Escobar

Published by The Entrepreneur's Bookshelf
ISBN: 979-8-9861039-0-7

No portion of this book may be reproduced or transmitted in any form or by any means-electronic, mechanical, photocopy, recording, or otherwise without the prior written permission of the copyright owner.

Dedication

I dedicate this book to my parents, Raul and Aracely Escobar. My parents are the reason I am the man I am today with a strong work ethic. My parents came to this country with no money, not knowing the English language at the time, but they never failed to provide for our family. Growing up (until I was about 10 years old), my siblings and I lived in a two-bedroom apartment with four boys in one room and our parents in the other. Can you imagine a room full of boys? It was a challenge, but we managed. We watched our parents work hard to keep a roof over our heads. My brothers and I never lacked love, protection, or food. We witnessed true love in a marriage, watching my parents happily married for close to 50 years now. My parents showed me how to go after my dreams, which I hold on to today.

Katie Escobar, my wife, I appreciate your support and encouragement, always believing in me. Now, I know you never married me for the money when we started. You married me for the "future money" you always knew one day would come (laughing moment). I honor you with this.

Thank you for allowing me the space and time to build on every dream I've ever had. You have not tried to hold me back from pursuing what I felt was a God-given vision. Thank you.

Noah, Zelie, Avila, Siena, and Judah, my children, know that your daddy loves you. And I want you to be inspired by my accomplishment of writing this book. I want you to know that anything is possible. With discipline, commitment, and dedication to your dreams, know that the sky's the limit. As your father, I will continue to lead by front and always strive to have you catch me in acts of excellence. I don't just want to tell you about hard work, discipline, and commitment; I want to show you.

Family and friends, there are not enough words to describe my whole heart, knowing that I've had your support thus far. Your commitment to me means more than you know. I hope this book makes you all proud. Finally, thanks to my past and present mentors, coaches, and trainers. You know who you are. I am forever grateful for how you've poured into me. I share my success and the impact I'm creating in this world with you.

Foreword

Throughout life, many of us experience thousands of unexpected first-time encounters with random strangers. Being a commentator and reporter that has covered the UFC and combat sports world for over 20-years, I have been blessed to travel the globe and experience many of these meetings, but it is impossible to remember them all. However, there is one random happenstance that I will never forget.

It took place while delayed in the George Bush Intercontinental Airport in Houston as I waited for a flight back home to Denver. A casual conversation with a stranger about a television show he enjoyed watching and one I used to work on called Inside MMA, on Mark Cuban's network AXS TV, led to a more in-depth dialogue about our mutual love and respect for the sport of mixed martial arts. Surprisingly, a simple 30-minute discussion on that normal Sunday morning eventually evolved into a sincere friendship and ongoing business relationship which I am fortunate to have today.

That random stranger in the Houston airport was entrepreneur and high-performance coach Jose Escobar. While I never imagined this random get-together with Jose would have such a positive impact on my life, I did realize immediately there was something unique, engaging and motivating about him. Once I learned he was a devoted martial artist that trained Brazilian Jiu Jitsu & Muay Thai, it became clear to me that he was a person who was driven for success, ambitious with his goals, and someone who could make a positive impact on anyone's professional and personal life.

As a husband for nearly 20 years and a father of three beautiful children myself, I was struck by what an incredible family man Jose is. He spoke about his wife Katie and his, then three, children, Noah, Zelie, and Avila, (since then they've welcomed their daughter Siena and new baby boy Judah) with incredible passion and love. And I realized right away Jose is the kind of family man I wanted to surround myself with.

In the highly competitive television industry where I have been fortunate to work since 1993, a successful person needs to be driven and goal-oriented and establish network connections with broadcast industry leaders. While I was able to accomplish many of those career goals myself, it was clear when Jose spoke about his role as CEO and Founder of The Connected Leaders Academy, and what the CLA was designed to do, that I could be doing so much more to further my career. Jose described the CLA as a TRIBE he created where entrepreneurs and business professionals come from around the world to grow personally and professionally, scale their influence, develop their skill sets, and ultimately grow their network. Those were all areas of the industry that were important to me and so I quickly became a proud member of the CLA "TRIBE".

I was honored when Jose asked me to be the inaugural keynote presenter at the MPower Virtual Global Summit and have the opportunity to speak with entrepreneurs from around the world and share my story. I never would have imagined that being a commentator for the sport of mixed martial arts would connect with so many business professionals, entrepreneurs, and members of MPower at the time.

Even though the pandemic spoiled the original in-person Summit and it had to go virtual, Jose and the team seamlessly transitioned all aspects of the meeting to online and it was an amazing success. Remarkably, he was able to have my former co-host from Inside MMA and UFC Hall of Famer, Bas Rutten, do a virtual seminar from his gym in Thousand Oaks, California to MPower members from around the world. His presentation on dedication and discipline in MMA and life in general (mixed in with some self-defense lessons as well) extraordinarily correlated with many of the MPower International Association Members.

Through the teachings of CLA and Jose Escobar, I truly believe I have accomplished more professionally, connected with more industry leaders, and had more career opportunities than ever before. By incorporating the lessons of the CLA, I have expanded my freelance broadcasting work and even scored a position with SuperBook Sports, hosting a show with NFL greats Ronde and Tiki Barber called "Betting with the Barbers". And this is just the beginning! I am thrilled to have been named one of the hosts for Jose's Connected Leaders Academy Global Summit in 2023.

This book *Winning the Day* is a guaranteed knockout that will teach entrepreneurs, business leaders, and all busy professionals how to create maximum productivity and balance in their morning and evening routine. After reading it, you will be able to implement a powerful system and learn customized morning and evening routines that will help you thrive both personally and professionally. If you are serious about becoming more productive, making more efficient use of your time, and creating a winning strategy mastering your AM and PM procedures, this is a must read.

Although he would probably pass on the opportunity, I'm fairly sure if I was to get Jose a fight in the UFC or the Legacy Fighting Alliance, he would be an instant fan favorite and leave the octagon with his arm raised in victory! He is a born winner and will succeed at any endeavor he puts his mind to. Enjoy this book and let's win the day together!

Ron Kruck

Content

Introduction

Chapter 1 The Transformation of 2019

Chapter 2 Winners Mindset

Chapter 3 The Morning Routine

Chapter 4 The Evening Routine

Chapter 5 The Power of Reading

Chapter 6 The Art of Journaling

Chapter 7 Commonplacing

Chapter 8 Examination of Conscience

Chapter 9 Personal Project Time

Closing

Acknowledgment

Introduction

Many people look at me now and see a much more polished version of who Jose Escobar used to be. They think I have it together with a perfect "not so little" family. While there are no significant issues in my marriage or family, what about my struggle? Success is often viewed only from an outward perspective. However, it has not always been as easy as it has looked for me. You will read about my success through the lens I wear.

As an adolescent growing into adulthood, I experienced some rough patches, actually many rough patches. I've placed myself in rocky situations where I didn't even reason with myself prior to putting myself in those settings. You may not believe this, but I have made many bad decisions that have ultimately landed me in jail. Not just once but on multiple occasions. Sorry to throw this jaw-dropping statement at you so soon, but I need my readers to understand that it wasn't always easy. Bar fights, house parties gone wrong, and numerous hospital visits (due to fights) led me to my martial arts journey. How's that for a connection?

I knew this could not be my final outcome. I was raised much better than this. It was time for a shift after a few jail visits, hospital stays, concussions, and stupid decisions. You can call me a late bloomer if you will. I didn't get serious about creating any real change until about eight years ago. That's when I committed to stopping my boy-like behavior and becoming a man. I didn't get married until I was 33 years old. That's when it hit me; it was time to find the courage and step it up.

My troubled mindset was not working for my good, which forced me to look at myself and make a life-changing decision. The most powerful question I asked was, how do I move forward? How do I take my family to a better place than they deserve? I knew immediately that I needed better habits and routines in place.

My morning and evening routine at the time had me feeling like I was going in circles and not accomplishing much. So, I began to change. I improved how I started my day. I made sure to take care of my physical body to help stimulate my mind. Once my workout was done first thing in the morning, I started making healthier choices regarding the food I would put in my body. I made it known that I was serious about fundamental transformation.

In February of 2017, I took a position with the Educational Funding Company (EFC) in Chevy Chase, Maryland. I was thrilled to work with this pioneer powerhouse company that has impacted the martial arts industry since 1967. I was making a name for myself with EFC in due time. By 2019, EFC noticed a significant shift in my work ethic and results. I would always remind my son, "Hard work always pays off!"

At this point, I was a business consultant with EFC and, as the months went on and I began to change, I showed up early and stayed late. I knew I was becoming different. On my lunch breaks, I would utilize that time to read a book, finish a chapter or start a new one. Co-workers didn't understand, but that was fine. I wasn't doing this for them, I was doing this for me. I was doing this for my family. I had tunnel vision.

I began to make a significant impact in the workplace and made a dent in the martial arts industry. It was so noticeable that EFC decided to promote me to a position that didn't even exist at the time. They created the sales director position and offered it to me. Let me pause to say this to you, if the work you seek doesn't exist, create it. Please don't wait for anyone to decide when it's your time, be the one to make it your time. My day job was not the only group noticing my transformation before their eyes. I was making it clear and known on my social media as well.

I wasn't on social media to see what everyone else was doing. Instead, I was on social media so everyone could see what I was doing. I was investing in myself. My daily postings were sending a different message. I was pulling back the curtains of my life and giving them the real and raw truth. I gave them an authentic perspective about my faith, family, business, health, and personal development. I stayed persistent and consistent with my posting, inspiring people to want to follow me and learn more.

Many paradigm shifts happened over the course of 2019. One of the main things that occurred was finally deciding to implement a morning and evening routine into my life. This addition to my life would quite literally elevate my game across the board. I leveled up across my ten life domains: spiritual, physical, financial, emotional, intellectual, vocational, avocational, marital, parental, and social.

Over the course of a decade before 2019, I had spent countless hours learning everything I could about the subject of morning and evening routines. I attended many seminars, webinars, masterminds, summits, and conventions. I listened to all the podcasts on the subject, and I watched hundreds of YouTube videos. I interviewed some of the best people and picked tons of successful people's brains on the topic. I was committed to developing mastery in this space.

As I continued to master my morning and evening routine, I hired a coach. Not just any coach, a multimillionaire who could help me launch a business. I began doing work with Tai Lopez and his team. I did extensive research on him and discovered he was the real deal. Working with Tai was one of the best decisions I ever made. Tai is a master in sales, marketing, social media, and many other things. I learned so much from him after taking a few of his courses.

I have always been a lifelong learner and not shy to invest in myself. Warren Buffett says it best, "The greatest investment one can make is an investment in themselves." Investing in Tai's programs was the right call at the time, for sure. Once I got my social media certification from Tai Lopez in 2019, I launched my first business, Fat Glass Marketing. It was a social media marketing agency in my chosen niche of restaurants and bars. I began to charge about $3000 USD per restaurant and bar to handle social media and drive traffic to their businesses. I had a videographer and photographer on staff to help with my content creation. I would create the ads, copy, hashtags, pixeling, targeting, retargeting, split testing ads, offers, etc. I took off in 2019, and the business was a success. Between my raise with EFC and my business, I doubled my income that year. I was determined to improve the quality of life for my family and make my parents proud.

I was finally beginning to develop this winner's mindset I've always been after. I continued to absorb information from the best all over the world. Another significant influencer who helped guide my path was Andy Frisella, author of "75 Hard." Although I had never met or worked with him, I decided to take on his program, 75 Hard. It's 75 days of challenging workouts (2 per day) and five other daily tasks with no days off. This program is designed to get a person mentally tough and disciplined. I completed the program successfully on my first attempt and lost over 36 pounds (keep in mind, 50 percent of those who try fail). Working out over time became a staple in my morning routine. Some call me crazy. Others call me committed.

I read a book weekly with this new mindset shift in my morning and evening routine. Yup! You read that correctly. I read one book a week, making that 52 books a year. How did I do it? How do I still to this day? I read every day for an hour. The intellectual stimulation was fantastic, and I was always thirsty for more. My lexicon began to expand like never before. I was quickly climbing that ladder to business success.

I had the one thing people sought after every day: energy. I spent more time with my family and learned to level up with them, not leave them out. I was feeling great. I began to deepen my spiritual life as well. I knew it was nothing but God's grace guiding me through this process of entrepreneurship. The doors were open for me; He showed me no man could shut them. I began to pray with purpose. Reading the Bible was now a daily habit. I took my family to Mass with me every Sunday. The Lord was very much the center of our home.

Emotionally, I was much more stable. My morning and evening routine helped with my inner peace and joy factor. The time I was taking for self-care translated into high levels of self-love. Financially, I was also in a better place. I learned better money management skills and started saving money and getting out of debt. I was on top of my finances, following a budget with my wife. I made sure bills for the business were being paid on time.

After seeing the results that happened in 2019 in my own life, I didn't want to keep it to myself. Curiosity kicked in, and I began to ask, "How can I teach this?" This question led to the birth of the second business I launched in 2020, "The Entrepreneur's Bookshelf." It's a digital programs company. I create courses and programs for busy professionals and entrepreneurs. My first digital program was "The Morning and Evening Routine Mastery." It took me two years to launch this program. Some call it, perfectionism. Others call it procrastination.

From 2019 to 2021, I was building and creating the program. During those years, I felt like I started over so many times. I was consistent with working on it but lacked execution on launching. I had delayed getting started due to procrastination, imposter syndrome, second-guessing myself, and lack of confidence. I was always finding one reason or another not to launch. The further I peeled the onion, the more I realized that I was caving into many limiting beliefs and automatic negative thoughts.

As I took time to reflect during my examination of conscience in my evening routine, I realized I lacked belief in myself. The truth of what was holding me back became more apparent. I was afraid of failure. I didn't want to disappoint my family and supporters. I didn't pull the trigger on launching my program until one day in 2021; I received the "one word" that turned my life around; EXECUTE!

I read the book *One Word* by Jimmy Page, Dan Britton, and Jon Gordon that year in 2021. This one-word concept helped change my life. The one word I chose for 2021 was "execute." I was determined to execute that year and launch my program once and for all. But I needed another expert to help, so I hired a coach. I paid a large sum to learn how to take what I knew and turn it into a program to sell. I finally launched my program in September 2021. In just 30 days of launching the program, I had made $28,000. This program has generated over $180K in less than a year since launching. Can you imagine if I had listened to my inner negative thoughts or those telling me I shouldn't invest so much money in a coaching program? I am beyond grateful that I decided to hire this coach and invest in his program. The Morning and Evening Routine Mastery program is taking off, and this is just the beginning. The secret to success lies in the bookends of your day.

My one word for the year 2022 was MONETIZE. On January 25, 2022, I launched my membership business called "The Connected Leaders Academy (CLA)." I thought of this idea the second week in January and launched it two weeks later on my birthdate. Within the first ten months of launching this new business, I enrolled over 225 paid members in 11 international countries and 34 states coast to coast nationwide. The tenth month generated over $22,000 in revenue in just that one month (my 2nd six figure business in under a year). Trust and believe this is only the beginning. By the end of 2023, I plan to have grown to over 1000 members making a global impact. Launching two multiple six-figure businesses in less than ten months with a full-time job and a family of 7 was no easy task. The ninja secret that allowed me to do this lies in the morning and evening routine. Let me give you an opportunity right now; if you want to grow personally and professionally and take your business to the next level, take my program, join my tribe and let's connect.

As you read this book, you will learn some tangible tips on leveling up your morning and evening routine. You will get a deeper insight into who I am and how I can help. Now get out your bookmark, highlighter, and pen. Engage the text and read on.

1
The Transformation of 2019

My years leading up to 2019 were destructive. Back then, I was constantly robbing Peter to pay Paul. Often not having a Peter but still a Paul to pay. I was completely in over my head. And I'm not talking about a couple thousand dollars either. I'm talking about tens of thousands.

Often, before we see the light at the end of the tunnel or the pot of gold on the other end of the rainbow, we feel the depths of destruction. And I felt every drop of rain that came through the storming thunder and lightning that was taking place in my life. Flooding, and I needed somebody to pass me a life jacket; I was sinking deep in shame.

I have never ever wanted, let alone desired, to live paycheck to paycheck. It must have been one of the worst experiences of my life. I found myself borrowing money before I knew I would have it to pay it back. Before the funds even touched the palm of my hand, they were already spent because it was never enough to catch me up.

Living behind the eight-ball in an awkward and uncomfortable position, one would look at my life before the transformation and say I was out of luck. I was barely making enough to provide for my family. Still, I tried my best never to come home with a look of defeat on my face. My wife saw me happy and believed I was managing our money well. I also thought I had everything under control, but the truth is I had nothing in control. In fact, I was completely out of control.

I became reckless with my spending. I wasn't a good financial planner before the transformation leading to 2019. My budgeting was *nonexistent*. If I wasn't as successful as I am today, I might not have the courage to tell this piece of my story, but my downfall is also a part of the puzzle that led me to success, so I'll continue to share it. As a matter of fact, if I'm going to help anyone with this book, I must share this part.

I had a terrible habit of paying off credit cards only to max them out again. Following that came the overdraft fees with my accounts. I'm fairly confident I donated a few thousand dollars, over the years, to my banks just in overdraft fees. I say this very sarcastically, of course. A donation I vow never to make again.

I recall, numerous times, calling customer service to fight and argue with whoever picked up the phone as if those fees were any of their responsibility. It had gotten so bad that they knew my name every time I called. They knew it was around the time and date that they should hear from me—such an embarrassing moment. A habit I couldn't break. Also, a practice I was doing nothing about but going in circles until it dizzied me out.

17

Physically, I became overweight. My average walk-around weight was 195 lbs.; I was standing at around 225 lbs. In addition to being obese, I was drinking myself happy. Happy hour meant just that for me, a time to drain all of my sorrows for the moment and be satisfied for an hour. I was eating every day like it was my last supper. I would find myself eating simply to pass the time. I was not doing anything intellectually. Reading, then, was nothing remotely close to how I read now. I would read about a book per quarter-four books a year (if I was lucky). You're shocked; I know since I now read over 52 books a year.

Emotionally, I was all over the place and messed up. The reality was that it would only get worse. Before the transformation, I was moody, short with my family, and not very engaged. The main thing that helped "fix" my emotional state was purchasing something. Just about anything, really. A book, however, was my preference.

Receiving purchases in the mail for me was the equivalent to the feeling a child would get at a candy store. Opening whatever I had purchased was fulfilling. I felt so good shopping with money I didn't have. I didn't concern myself with balancing the checkbook before making a purchase. I did what I wanted and how I wanted to do it without checking in with anyone.

Spiritually, I was okay. At least, I thought I was. I believed in God and had a strong faith, but I wasn't living my faith as I should have been. I was fully aware that my circumstances were on me and my choices, not God's. My poor habits had me shackled to mediocrity and frustration. While I did attend Mass every Sunday, before the transformation of 2019, I would attend Mass only because my wife wanted me to. It wasn't something I truly wanted for myself. I just knew it was the right thing to do. I would read my Bible occasionally without desiring any specific comprehension, it was simply to check it off my to-do list.

As a husband, I was average. At this moment, I think maybe I was below average. I was there for my wife and kids, but I had no energy to play with them. I felt lazy, and I was lazy. I just wanted to smoke my cigar, drink a cold beer, and not accept or embrace that I was living a lie and I was not fully transparent with my family. What a lame and horrible place to be.

Then, I stumbled upon a book, *Your Best Year Ever* by Michael Hyatt. In this life-changing book, he talks about the ten life domains:

1. Spiritual

2. Intellectual

3. Emotional

4. Physical

5. Marital

6. Parental

7. Social

8. Vocational

9. Avocational

10. Financial

After reading this book and a few notable others like *The 5 AM Club* by Robin Sharma and *The Miracle Morning* by Hal Elrod, I decided it was time to implement everything I had learned for over a decade. I felt that mindset shift within. I will never forget it. The night before January 1, 2019, I sat my wife down to have a conversation that would change everything. I shared that I would commit to a morning and evening routine for the entire year of 2019 with no excuses, zero compromises, high-level discipline, and extreme ownership.

The more I read and put all the pieces of the puzzle together (again, over a decade of research), the more I realized that the most successful business leaders in the world generally have a morning and evening routine. The commonality encouraged me to join the club. I woke up on this new mission with a rise-and-grind mentality. There was a renewed work ethic and newfound vigor in me to seek this self-mastery I longed for. I interviewed some of the best entrepreneurs and attended many seminars, masterminds, and paid mentorships. I was devouring information on another level, and I loved it.

 I was no longer spinning out of control and making poor choices. I stopped making multiple random unnecessary purchases just to fill a void only God could fill. I discontinued drinking my "adult beverages" most of the week. I was now implementing the keys to success that I was always reading about, and I was fully committed to this process. There was no turning back. I had to do it.

I implemented 5 am workouts to start my mornings. This was a non-negotiable Monday through Friday. In doing that, I left no room for procrastination and excuses. I was laser-focused on the ten life domains and achieving real transformation across the board. I had it firm in my heart that this was my time. I watched myself change day after day.

One of the most notable changes of this journey was in the finances. Now I was coming into my transformation as I doubled my income, received a raise at my job (through my promotion to Sales Director), launched my first business from scratch, and grew my influence like never before. I had lost a significant amount of weight (over 36 pounds) and improved my marriage, becoming that trophy husband (at least, I think so). Then, my wife and I attended a seminar that brought us closer together. It was held by Gary Chapman, the author of the classic book *The 5-Love Languages*. This is a must-read for any married couple, I highly recommend.

Additionally, I became a better father to my kids and my social life was improving as I leveled up my circle. I even created more time to do things I enjoyed, like martial arts and stogies with friends over coffee.

The transformation I was experiencing in 2019 was not only healthy but also freeing. I was now seventy percent out of debt, making more money than ever before. With my income rising, I was strong-minded in staying the course of paying down my debt with no intention of abusing any limits on my credit cards. My wife and I were careful to follow the system from Dave Ramsey's book, *The Total Money Makeover*. The winner's mindset was now elevated to the 2.0 version of myself. Life was at an all-time high at the end of 2019. Every change that had occurred, I owed to the morning and evening routine system I developed and put in place.

2
Winner's Mindset

As Jim Rohn stated, we become the average of the five people we spend most of our time with. With a statement like that, we must protect and consider our circle carefully. Look around; who do you hang out with? Could you have chosen more wisely? Are you around takers all the time and those who may drag you down? You should be around givers and those who will pour into you.

It's imperative that you do not allow anyone to plant negative seeds in your mind. We must become the greatest gatekeepers of our minds. The mindset we establish distinguishes between a winner and a loser's mindset. How we cultivate our minds will either lead us to success or cause us to experience more failures than we desire.

With whom you spend your time truly does matter. Many times your circle is the difference-maker in how you show up in life and business. Don't allow negative people with negative mindsets to build around you. Sometimes all it takes is one person you carry around with a negative mindset to ruin your dreams and goals without you even realizing it. My goal for you is to help develop the winner's mindset in you. My goal is to bring alive those grand ideas you once had. That imagination someone told you was absurd. I'm here to bring that back out of you. I'm here to break the chains of strongholds that have held you down for far too long.

Developing a winner's mindset is not easy. One must be deliberate in taking the necessary steps to plant the right thoughts on fertile soil. Since the beginning stages of creating a winner's mindset can be unpredictable, you must position yourself for success. Being mindful of how much television you watch can also help develop a winner's mindset. You may have to exchange your favorite TV series for a book. You may have to slow down on binge-watching to hear the following audio that could change and save your life. Positioning a winner's mindset is having to do a double take. Looking back, realizing what didn't work; laziness, excuses, poor habits, late nights with friends, having too much fun, and yet not being willing to pay the price once the high wore off.

A winner's mindset begins with being honest with yourself. Take extreme ownership and accountability for where you are now. This is a direct result of the mindset you have been operating from. A winner's mindset remains consistent even in discomfort. Grab a pen and write this down: *My goals and dreams lie outside of my comfort zone. I must LIVE in my discomfort zone.*

Why did I ask you to write this down? Because I need you to start stretching your thoughts, ideas, and mind like a rubber band. A rubber band, once stretched, never goes back to its original dimensions. Author and speaker (now one of my mentors), John Maxwell talks about this all the time. Everything we do daily is operated by thought. So, if I can help you by focusing and positioning your mind to think great things, then your mind will no longer settle for mediocrity and the status quo that most people lay down for.

Our minds only know what we feed it, give it negativity, and it will dish out negativity. If negativity hangs around too long, it will become a stronghold in our lives, making it more difficult to break loose. You must pause at some point and internalize where you see yourself in 5 years' time. Have you asked yourself that question, "Where do I see myself in 5 years?" I believe three factors determine this:

1- With whom you spend your time

2- Where you spend your money
3- What books you are reading

These three factors listed above, if not reflected upon regularly, could have you in the presence of misery. As the saying goes, "misery loves company." You must determine if you will partake in a fixed or growth mindset.

A fixed mindset means that you believe your mental abilities and IQ are fixed (set, unchanging, permanent), therefore staying stagnant. If you are an average thinker, then you will always be average. If you are not strong in one area of your life and choose not to grow, you will remain the same. A growth mindset means believing you can always be more, do more, and have more. A growth mindset understands the power of evolution. The bigger you can think, the more you can achieve. I believe the two are interconnected when it comes to a growth mindset.

A winner's mindset is one of positivity, abundance, and expectancy. Always seeking growth! Always pressing for more while embracing discomfort. Brazilian Jiu-Jitsu Black Belt and Mindset Coach, Chris Matakas states, "You are only as strong as your environment demands you to be." This directly means that life only improves when you get better! It's not up to your circumstances or surroundings rather it's up to you to constantly evolve and improve. Your thoughts have tremendous weight on what happens in life. It's been said that your thoughts become words, your words become actions, your actions become habits, and over time, those habits become your character which seals your destiny.

A winner's mindset is where it all begins. Will it always be a stroll through a tulip garden? No! Of course not. You may trip up here and there and create a little mess from time to time but be a person of action. Obstacles will come. As Ryan Holiday titled it in his book, *The Obstacle is the*

Way: The Timeless Art of Turning Trials into Triumph. You, as you're reading this, must not try to walk around it or hide from it. Embrace it and take it on!

You have the ability to carry on the thoughts that create the momentum to win. Stacking wins after time builds success. There is a real compound effect to win stacking. But you have to push and go hard in everything you do. The bank accepts cash and check deposits all day. One thing you cannot deposit in your bank account is excuses. This means you have to put in the work. The work yields results. However, the results only come if you don't make excuses. Excuses won't make you any money to deposit in the bank. You either get the job done or you don't. Nobody has time or energy for your excuses. There are tiers to life and each tier is going to require a better and different version of yourself. Your mindset must not be fixed but stirred to constant growth.

Growth doesn't just happen; growth is intentional.

3
The Morning Routine

The morning routine is how you start your day. You decide the moment your feet touch the ground if you will win the day and take it on or start with a big fat "L" on your forehead. Every morning when I wake up, I decide to win. I take control of my day, starting as early as 4 AM. While the pets are sleeping, family is still in bed, no one's texting or pulling for my attention, and no one is on social media, I get up to get my day started.

    This discipline of getting up is not based on a "when I feel like it" schedule. It is my Monday through Friday 4 AM sharp schedule. No compromise. I'm not negotiating with sleep. I'm not trying to come up with an alternative. I get up. To anyone who says, "I am not a morning person," let me help you to change your language. My advice would be, it's not that you are not a morning person. You simply don't prefer it because you may not be used to it. But anything done repeatedly becomes a habit. You can become a morning person if you choose to.

No one enjoys the strong taste of coffee the very first time they try it. Perhaps with the right amount of cream and sugar it will grow on you. I like to call this an acquired taste. Very much like a fine wine or smooth stogie, your taste buds start to familiarize themselves with what you are consuming and acquire a liking for it. Same idea with creating a morning routine when you are not a morning person. It will eventually grow on you. The incremental change will allow you to adapt over time.

You must consistently invest in yourself to keep up with the top 3%. Who are the top 3%? You've all heard of Bill Gates, Oprah, Warren Buffet, Elon Musk, and Mark Zuckerberg. Sure, you may be saying they are billionaires, but it didn't start that way for any of them. Before they became millionaires and billionaires, they were getting up early with a morning routine.

You must not fall into formation with others in life who only move and take action when life forces them to. If you are not hard on yourself, life will do you that favor by default. You set the tone for your life. Stop waiting on the sidelines and get in the game. Be proactive and create the life you want. Let the winner's mindset set your sail and press you to wake up early.

Let me tell you about my five-second rule. And no, this does not mean eating something that just fell on the floor within five seconds. This rule states that you have five seconds to get up out of bed once your alarm clock goes off for your morning routine. Once five seconds pass, your brain will automatically start to negotiate why you don't need to wake up and make excuses for sleeping in or a bit longer. Do not, under any circumstances, hit the snooze button.

This is how I wake up on time and efficiently:

- My alarm goes off (on the opposite side of the room) and I immediately stand up in less than five seconds.
- I walk over to turn off my alarm with no regrets or thoughts of going back to bed
- I turn on the bright light in my bathroom
- Wash my face with freezing cold water
- Brush my teeth and use a tongue scraper
- Urinate to empty my bladder
- Weigh myself (best time to do it every day for accuracy)
- Put on my sneakers (I wear my gym clothes to bed)
- Exit the room and start my morning routine

If you snooze, you lose! Don't let it happen.

Was getting up easy at first? No. But I had to train myself and my mind by feeding it reasons why I needed to get up early. Bestselling author and one of the world's top leadership experts, Robin Sharma stated, "Many want the rewards of world-class but don't want to embrace the requirements to world-class." I knew I couldn't be one of them, the one classified as wanting success and rewards without wanting to do any work or make any effort. I began to take myself, my well-being, and my success seriously. I knew I had to pour into myself first each and every day. I had to believe in myself first before I could ever expect anyone else to believe in me.

As I said, having a morning routine is critical. I want you to think about how you start and end your day. Many understand that how we start our day is a significant factor in completing it, yet it's rarely taken seriously. Write this down, *Learning the art of **my** morning routine will show me who I am.* See that the word *my* is bolded, indicating it's personal.

Everything you do will start small before it grows. You may begin by getting up just 15 minutes earlier than usual, then gradually move to 30 minutes, then 45 minutes, and then an hour. The mind will start to tap into this new habit that you are starting to form, and it will adapt to the change. You will get so used to getting up early to start your morning routine that you won't even need an alarm. Your body will naturally begin to wake up because it knows the morning routine. Incremental change is the key so that it is sustainable over time.

The truth is, we can't afford to sleep in. We must be the first to take the W (win) for the day. How you show up for yourself matters. If you've made it this far in the book, you are ready to commit to a new wake-up time. I have shared with you that 4 AM is my time. What will be your wake-up time? Write it down below on the line provided and then sign or place your initials by the time.

Just this small task will have a domino effect on everything else. Pay close attention to your morning routine. Keep in mind that on average it takes 66 days to implement a new habit to the point where it hits the stage of automaticity. So, don't expect change overnight. Give yourself grace along the way. Remember, how you start the first hour of your day is critical. It's not so much about just waking up early. What exactly are you doing with your time? How are you spending your first few hours after you get up? Let me remind you that the mind, body, soul, and heart need to be filled first thing in the morning.

Let's tackle the morning.

4
The Evening Routine

Have you ever taken the time in the evenings to look over what you've accomplished during the day? If we would just pause in the evening, we could tell if we've been aligned with our assignments for the day, or if we've been caught slacking off. What I want you to understand is that your evening routine, along with mine, should be used to reflect on the day's wins or losses, if any.

You may be asking why you should reflect on your wins and losses and the answer is simple. Reflection gives us an opportunity to see where we might have gone wrong. It gives us the space to better ourselves without any judgment and challenges us to better prepare for the next day. Without a sense of reflection, one will never make the changes needed to grow. During your time of reflection in the evening, you can better plan for tomorrow.

Why is your evening routine so essential? Well, considering I just discussed the importance having a morning routine, I'll add that the best morning routine begins the night before. Knowing what needs to be accomplished before the start of your day allows you to rest better at night. Think about it, people often go to bed with countless never-ending thoughts running through their minds. With a to-do list that seems too impossible to get done in just 24 hours. If you begin to shift your way of thinking, you will sleep better. This is a method I practice every night. I brainwash myself with positive affirmations that motivate me and mentally prepare me for the next morning.

Moreover, I don't allow myself to become overwhelmed before going to bed. Instead, I use my evenings to decompress. The purpose of my evenings is to relieve and reduce any pressure that the day has placed on me. It's necessary to balance your emotions and feelings before ending the night. Remember, your best mornings are indicative of the actions taken the night before. In other words, how you end your night will be how you start your morning.

In contrast, your worst mornings are also indicative of the actions you took the night before. If you go to bed overwhelmed, you'll wake up overwhelmed. If you go to bed angry, you'll most likely wake up angry. However, if you go to bed in peace, you'll wake up in peace. Keep this strategy in mind and never "squeeze in" one more email when you know you don't have the mental capacity to entertain it and answer it appropriately. A method I use is to never open an email unless I am ready to fully respond. And I encourage you to take on some of these methods if you struggle with the feeling of having to answer right away. Trust me, answering the message in the morning is just fine.

Instead, you should use that time to journal. Place all your concerns or ideas on paper, releasing them from your mind. Doing this one small task will relieve you from staying up later than expected. When emotions are released it feeds the body a clearer thought process and reduces tension in the body and brings about a greater self-awareness of anything that you may have written down because you're able to see it from a different perspective.

Take Notes

Not only do you want to manage your last activity before going to bed but you also want to ensure that you are not just allowing time to pass. Alternatively, you should allow time to be on your side. How? You may ask. When you position yourself to win, not only do you change your mindset but there's also an internal time clock that ticks second by second, tick tock, tick tock. With every tick and every tock, you must be sure to position yourself to receive the benefits of an evening routine.

Benefits

- *Improve memory*
- *Feel happier*
- *Stimulate weight loss*
- *Muscle recovery*
- *Better sleep quality*
- *Reduce the risk of any health disease*
- *Strengthen immune system*
- *Reduce anxiety*
- *Reduce depression*
- *Feel more energized*
- *Feel more confident about self*
- *More alert*
- *More focus*
- *More productive*

All these things take place from going to bed at a reasonable time.

Let's shift for a moment because there's something critical that takes place in the evenings and, if not careful, it can get the best of an individual. It's called bedtime procrastination. Bedtime procrastination is putting off going to bed for no good reason. Essentially doing mundane and unnecessary tasks just to stay up. Perhaps just passing time by binging on Netflix or something would also qualify. To avoid bedtime procrastination, you must, and I emphasize *MUST,* set your evenings to align with your daily schedule. Putting things off to either handle "tomorrow" or over the "weekend" pushes you back from personal growth and development.

    Your evening routine should permit you to move the needle of success closer in your direction. Let me explain, if anything you're set to do distracts or pulls the needle of success further away from you, then it's safe to say that a mental shift must take place in order for alignment to take place.

    You will always tell when your evening routine is in place properly because, to start, your time will be used wisely. Your television won't become the focus of the evening, social media platforms will be shut down for the night, and all phone calls will be sent to voicemail. And, while those things are in place, you should find yourself doing these instead:

- Researching information to grow your business or brand
- Preparing speeches in the event you get called for a speaking opportunity
- Managing your budget to ensure your funds are being spent accordingly
- Creating the next program to 10X your business
- Creating and developing business proposals
- And constantly moving the needle of success in your direction

To ensure I have the proper atmosphere once I transition from my evening routine to my bedtime routine, I make certain to have a few things in order in my bedroom alone.

My personal list is as follows, (your list may differ from mine):

- Black-out curtains
- Lowered temperature for a more comfortable sleeping experience (purchase a fan if needed)
- Earplugs for noise elimination
- Comfortable bedding
- Prayer which is always in order

Having these things in place helps me in completing my bedtime routine because it allows me to fall into a peaceful rest when I lay my head. In my evening routine, I set aside two hours, specifically between 8:30pm-10:30pm. This two-hour window allows me to focus on preparing for the next day. As I mentioned before, I also take this time to go over my own wins and losses during the day. I reflect on what went wrong or what went right, and what I can do to ensure a better tomorrow.

In creating a bedroom environment that is conducive to a good night's rest (nothing sexual here), the mood ought to be taken into consideration. Our bodies associate themselves with the environment and the energy we feed it. The bed should be kept solely as your resting place. If your bed becomes associated with social media, checking emails, texting, making late-night calls, and eating snacks, then once you're in the bed, instead of resting the body, it will want to do one of the activities I've just mentioned.

If you're not ready to physically lay down and call it a night, try checking last-minute emails in the living room. Keep as much, if possible, out of the bedroom so you use that place only for resting. Will this be an easy task? Absolutely not. Will it take some discipline? Yes. But I can assure you when you do not bring your laptop, iPad, or computer into your bedroom you sleep much better. The only tech I have in my room is my cell phone, but it's put down charging on the opposite side of the room. If your home office happens to be in your bedroom (mine once was) just make sure to shut everything completely off once your evening routine is done and your bedtime routine begins.

Something else you may want to keep in mind is how you're setting your bedtime hour. I know what you are thinking, 'I'm a grown man or woman, I don't need to set a bedtime hour.' However, that couldn't be further from the truth. Planning your hours of rest prepares you for an early and productive rise. As Benjamin Franklin stated, "Early to bed and early to rise makes a man healthy, wealthy, and wise."

When there is no structure in your evening routine, you will find yourself scrolling the web for items you don't need or never thought of until you saw a commercial for them. We do this more in our evenings when the day is less stressful and less packed with errands. If you don't believe me, check your bank statements. What are the hours you tend to spend the most? If your evenings are taking a hit with your spending, you may want to give yourself a spending limit for the week or even the day (budgets will differ).

Taking the necessary time to budget in the evening will help keep you in line as it keeps me from spending money I don't have or have but not for "that" online item. And if you're one that doesn't enjoy shopping online like the rest of us, this same principle applies when you take a trip to the mall. Our minds begin to play tricks on us as soon as we swing open those entry doors to the mall. Immediately, we start feeling like we "deserve" to purchase something. We feel like we deserve to spoil ourselves. Or we deem it "self-care." While there is nothing wrong with indulging and treating ourselves from time to time, the point I am making here is that it needs to be within the budget. Managing your evening budget will allow you to make better decisions now and tomorrow.

I know I've said a mouthful in this chapter but let me leave you with a few more evening routine pointers. How you conduct your evening routine will show you one of two things. It will show you just how productive you are (by what you get done). Or it will show you how unproductive you are by chasing or completing the non-urgent things in life. Time is precious. It's the one thing we all fight against, and the thing we'll never get back.

We must all make a decision today not to let time pass us by. We cannot become so busy that we can't recall what we've actually accomplished. A busy body is one that thinks he or she is productive with no meaning or purpose to what they are actually doing. During your evening routine, I want you to closely monitor yourself. Is there always a beer in your hand? Is a glass of wine consistently your go-to? Is your iPad your safe haven? No judgment. I just want us to hold each other accountable. Keep in mind, the less you get done in the evening, the more you put on yourself for the morning.

One last golden nugget before I move on, I encourage you to stop watching television and scrolling through your phone for at least an hour before going to bed. Many may not be aware of this but the blue light from your screen(s) disrupts your sleeping pattern. You see, our brain is aware of night and day, light and darkness. So, when it sees light it knows to stay awake. When it senses darkness, it also knows it's time for bed.

Constantly scrolling through your phone and watching a great deal of television begins to confuse the mind. When it thinks it's time for bed because it's late in the evening, but you're stimulating it with bright lights, sounds, and images, you begin to train the brain to stay awake when it should be resting. Now if you just absolutely have work to do and it can't wait until tomorrow then consider purchasing Gunnar Glasses. These glasses have been designed to block out blue light. It's good for gamers, iPad readers, and computer users.

  Experts suggest we place our phones away from our reach in the evenings to ensure a good night's rest. Our evening routine ought to get us excited for the next morning. Our bedtime hour must make sense in conjunction with our wake-up time. We cannot expect to have a fun-filled morning at 6:00am when we are going to bed at midnight. Begin to change and adjust your evening sleeping pattern to better fit and accommodate your morning routine. The two-work hand in hand.

  Start off in small increments when adjusting to a new evening routine. Trying to make a drastic change will cause you to lose interest in the change quicker than when you first started. If you're going to bed late and you have early mornings, try going to bed 15 minutes earlier than usual. Then push your bedtime to 30 minutes earlier than usual until you are comfortable calling it a night at 10:00pm or 10:30pm instead of one or two in the morning. But remember, start now, start today, and start in increments.

5
The Power of Reading

*The man who does not
read good books has no advantage
over the man who cannot read
~Mark Twain*

For as long as I can remember, I have always been intrigued by books. The information they held; the different categories; the genres of fiction, nonfiction, novels; and, most of all, the smell of the book's spine. Yes, I take a book and, as weird as it may sound, I smell the spine. Now I don't do this to every random book, but definitely to every new book I purchase. However, let's move on.

As a kid, I enjoyed flipping through the pages of the books in our school library. I was that kid, the one that hung out in the library, getting lost in mountains of books. I was such a bookworm. When there were book fairs in school, you could count on me to be at every one. In fact, I enjoyed checking books out of the library just to check them back in after reading them, knowing I would only be checking out another one.

Reading gave me a sense of purpose. The more I learned, the more I felt like I could accomplish anything I set out to do. For the most part, reading has been the needle mover in my life, but not always. Something happened in my second year of college, and I was getting sidetracked from my daily reads. I found myself at more parties than I had desired, getting caught up in having that "college experience." I took it too far, and the needle to success began to drift in the opposite direction.

Without notice, I was changing. I wasn't as peaceful or joyful throughout the day when I stopped reading, instead I was dealing with headaches and hangovers. I never truly realized how much positive power reading actually had over me, power that I was now losing because of the choices I made. I didn't like how I was beginning to feel. I wanted my joy back. I wanted my peace back. So, I began to read again this time with intention.

Fast forward to 2019 and I was back on track. I started reading a book a week. I had everyone lined up, ready to soak in what I could; John Maxwell, Robert Greene, Ryan Holiday, Cal Newport, Seth Godin and my list went on. My passion for reading had returned. And for every *one* book I read, I would purchase five more. Primarily reading self-help, business, personal development books (90 percent nonfiction). That's how devoted I had become to taking back my life, knowledge, and purpose. I wasn't going into this with the same mindset I had previously. This time, I became more concerned with the books I had surrounding me. I didn't mind trading brand clothes for books. I was so focused on my growth that I kept telling myself, "You won't buy expensive things without a ticket to a seminar."

Austin Phelps said it best, "Wear the old coat and buy the new book." We've gotten so caught up in the latest new clothes, shoes, and trends that we focus more on our outer appearance than we do our minds. I would rather buy the book. I would rather be at the next 10X Growth Conference with Grant Cardone. I would rather sign up for a mastermind or hire a business mentor because I know that the investment I'm making will have a higher return. It's all about keeping the main thing the main thing.

I can't help but continue quoting the legends because I need you to understand the point I'm making here regarding books. This quote also rings true, "A room without books is like a body without a soul" -Marcus Tullius Cicero. I feel empty when I don't read. I feel like I've done myself a disservice when I don't take the time to open up the pages of the book that might lead me to my new idea. I'm a true reader. I don't always read a book once and be done. I'm what they call a re-reader. I will read, if necessary, the same book twice (assuming it's a goodie).

There's a section in my home library that is categorized solely for my re-reads. As a matter of fact, there are sections for almost anything you could think of: must-reads, masterpieces, references, and more. Every time I walk into my home library it responds to me in a different way. Depending on what's going on in my day or how I am feeling at the moment, my room of books may hit either a spiritual or mental cord. Sitting silently amongst my books helps me redirect my thoughts to more positive and energetic thoughts. My library is my personal gift to myself that I use to gift to others as well.

I believe gifting a book to someone is the most powerful gift they could receive. I make sure to pull out my heavy hitters when debating which book I should give because I value the power of a book. I teach to never just read as an activity on your to-do list. Don't just read because you may have a paper due, you're preparing for a speech, or you have a last-minute training call and you need something to reference. Read because you know it will stimulate the mind like a muscle and the brain will grow, so we must water it daily with new knowledge and wisdom.

Show me a family of readers and I will show you the people who move the world (Napoleon Bonaparte). That is the power of reading. The world belongs to those who have a large worldview and get educated through reading books. The more you know, the more you do with what you know. Reading specific things can and will make a difference in your life. The highest performers in life, the CEOs of Fortune 500 companies will tell you all the same thing.

Love them or hate them, doesn't matter. It's a proven fact that the average CEO reads about 60 books a year. Here are some high performers both past and present that are avid readers just to name a few:

- *Abraham Lincoln*
- *Winston Churchill*
- *Queen Elizabeth*
- *Albert Einstein*
- *Warren Buffett*
- *Bill Gates*
- *Lebron James*
- *Oprah Winfrey*
- *Elon Musk*
- *Mark Zuckerberg*
- *Mark Cuban*

The list could go on, but I will spare you. There you have it, a short list of our high-level readers of both past and present. The question you must ask yourself is are you among the greats? Are you a high-level reader, are you average, are you below average? Believe it or not, we all fall under a specific category.

When it comes to reading, there are three tiers known as milestones which help to place us properly. Read carefully to view your position in one of the following tiers. Don't be so quick to place yourself under any tier. A high-level reader doesn't happen overnight. Sometimes a high-level reader is birthed out of a nonreader, someone who absolutely dislikes picking up a book to read.

First Milestone

Be sure to read EVERY DAY! How much you read doesn't matter. Just get in the habit of picking up a book and reading for two, five or even 15 minutes. The goal is to get you into reading and out of bad habits. I always go for a physical book over audio or kindle. There is something special about a physical book versus an audio. It's like the difference between free weights and machines. Get a physical book every day and read. You may surprise yourself. Two, five, or even 15-minute reading times can lead to an hour over time. Start today.

Second Milestone

Commit to reading ten pages a day no matter what. I'm talking about no matter how crazy your day has been. No matter how many co-workers found a way to annoy you. No matter how loud the children are screaming when you get home. Read ten pages a day no matter what. Do you know how many books you will read in a year's span if you commit to this? Eighteen! You could be on your way to reading eighteen books a year by reading ten pages a day from a book that averages 200 pages. This is a great start for a person who doesn't like to read. It could actually be a game-changer for you.

Third Milestone

Read for 45-minutes every day. If the book has around 150 pages and you're an average reader, that's about a book a week. Making that 52 books a year. Imagine how many books you could get through if you read for 1-hour a day?

Reading is power, but it's a tool that requires much attention and discipline. I tell people all the time that, if you want it bad enough, you'll do whatever it takes to attain it. So, if you want the skill of reading to become a habit, you will begin with either tier one, tier two, or tier three. Either way, you'll get started today.

I personally read 30-minutes in my morning routine and another 30-minutes in my evening routine. That's one hour a day that I set aside to read, grow, and gain new wisdom, knowledge, and understanding. It may require that I adjust my time with certain things but nonetheless, it's an hour a day. And I never put reading to the side as something to do "later." That is the worst habit you could get yourself caught up in.

You must set your priorities for the day the night before and then, get it done. If, for whatever reason, I can't squeeze in two 30-minute reading sessions, then I do what I call the 20-20-20 rule. That's 20 minutes in the morning, 20 minutes in any gap I can find in my day (perhaps lunch time), and 20 minutes in the evening. I find the 20 minutes to get it done without excuses.

Famous Italian writer Umberto Eco has one of the fullest home libraries one can imagine. His home consists of over 30,000 books. When he died, he left what was described as a vast collection of books. Do you think he read them all? Absolutely not. His home library wasn't about reading and getting through all of his books, rather it was about keeping him curious, and his mind stimulated enough to know that it can always learn and know more.

I'm not sharing this for you to go out and build yourself a 30,000-built-in home library. I am simply suggesting that you check to see what you have in your personal library as it should be used as a research tool as well. In any section of your books, you should be able to find what you need in your own home. If you cannot find the book that is needed then begin building your home library just one book at a time.

I've surrounded my home office with books because they keep me humble. It reminds me of how little I know and makes me feel powerful knowing I'm surrounded by so much knowledge. I'm hungry to learn. I have over 2,500 books but that's not enough. The goal is to have 10,000 books available to me at any time right at the tip of my fingers. Let me prepare myself for what's to come when I build this 10,000-book home library and I hope this helps you prepare too for when you encounter this situation. At that point, I'll know my haters by their fruits, they will begin to sound like this, "And how many of those 10,000 books have you read?" In turn, I will kindly answer them, "It's not about how many I've read, but how I use them."

There's no doubt I'll reach my goal of 10,000 books, as you've read, for every-one book I read, I purchase five. I'm on track to reading 60-70 books a year. It's not to prove anyone wrong or right. I do this for my own personal development because I'm thirsty for knowledge, I can't stay in the same place. I'm always on to next-level thinking. The moment I start believing that I know it all will be the beginning of my own downfall.

Here are some benefits that reading can have in your life:

- Mental Stimulation
- Stress Reduction
- Gained Knowledge
- Expansion of Vocabulary
- Better Concentration
- Better Writing Skills
- Memory Expansion

- Improved Brain Power
- Longer Life
- Regained Focus
- Relaxation

People tend to say, knowledge is power. I say "applied knowledge" is power. Head knowledge is not enough. When I read books, I stop and use my stand-by dictionary to identify words with which I am unfamiliar. I use my pen to underline the word. Then I take the word, place it on an index card on one side, and on the other, I define the word followed by creating a sentence with the word. This is my strategy for learning new words. For many, this may be considered "too much." And that's okay, I'm simply sharing my method and what helps me expand in knowledge.

After the words are on index cards, I go through them as if I am back in high school or middle school trying to learn words for a spelling bee. Reading is power and I consider myself an active reader versus a passive reader. In all my years of reading, I have realized there are differences between the two. Keep in mind everything under the "active readers" list is what I personally do.

<u>Active Reader</u>

- Engage with the text
- Write within the margins of the book
- Underline the text
- Highlight sentences
- Write down ideas
- Disagree with the Author
- Fold pages
- Make references
- Make notes of key takeaways
- Make note of the most valuable piece of information learned

- Create an index in the front of the book with most valuable pieces of information

Getting serious about reading is one of the greatest ways to reach success, financial freedom, and gain wisdom. Every book has about 30-40% of meat and golden nuggets attached to it, the rest is just filler words (generally speaking). But that doesn't matter because it's what you do with that 30-40% that will pave the way for a successful life and/or business.

 Reading may not come as naturally to some, as it does for me, but it takes practice. I naturally enjoy reading but I would also consider myself to be a slow reader. How fast you read is irrelevant. Just read! You must make reading become a habit for you as you would with eating, showering, and brushing your teeth. Sounds so simple when it's put that way but I want you to think about it. How many children fight with their parents to brush their teeth, get in the shower, and eat their vegetables? Still, over time the child knows that doing these three things is more beneficial for them than it is for their parents.

Another piece of advice I would give concerning reading is to get in the habit of carrying a book with you. Have one in the car, one in your locker at work, keep one in your bag or purse. I have gotten in the habit of having a book in hand everywhere I go. I call it an everyday carry, just like my wallet, keys, and cell phone. I'm reading while waiting for my son when picking him up from school or at my dentist's waiting room. At the gym or during my lunch break, I make time to read. That's how much reading has become important to me. Reading is power!

When people say, "I don't have time to read," I tell them it's not a matter of time, it's a matter of priority and finding the right book. They are simply reading books they don't like which doesn't keep their focus. If you don't like the book you're reading, move on to the next one. Simple! It's okay to start a book and put it down once you realize the book is just not catching hold of your focus or attention. Additionally, I tell others to keep a book close by. It's always good to have reading material with you. If you're reading from your phone, place the phone on airplane mode so you're not distracted by incoming calls, text messages, or social media alerts. You can also take a trip to the library or bookstore. Add that to your calendar as something you must do. You must surround yourself with books to know if you really have time to read or not.

    We have to make reading a priority and non-negotiable. After all, it's free (in a way). Whether you're a nonreader or reader, start off by checking out free books from the library. Not every book needs to be purchased. While it may be good to own the book in the future, if you're just starting off, check out books from your nearest library.

It's free entertainment with unlimited resources. Ultimately, everyone has to start somewhere.

The benefits of reading are endless. We must brainwash ourselves with sayings that may not be true now but over time and with repetition, those words come true; "I love to read, and I am a strong reader. I can read a paperback, hardcover, and even from a kindle. I can do anything I set my mind to do, and reading is one of them." You must affirm yourself and repeat this daily, even when you don't feel it if you're serious about becoming an active reader.

If you're struggling to know with whom to start, below I have provided a list of just a few of my favorite authors:

- Robin Sharma
- John Maxwell
- Ryan Holiday
- Robert Green
- Jocko Willink
- Cal Newport
- C. S Lewis

- Michael Hyatt
- Timothy Ferriss
- Grant Cardone
- Seth Godin
- Malcolm Gladwell
- Jordan B. Peterson
- Matthew Kelly
- Brian Tracy
- Dan Kennedy
- Brendon Burchard
- Scott Hahn
- Dan Lok
- Jared Diamond
- Mark Manson
- Simon Sinek
- Zig Ziglar
- Hal Elrod
- Dave Kerpen
- Austin Kleon
- Jim Collins
- Donald Miller
- Robert T. Kiyosaki
- T.D. Jakes
- Tony Robbins

When any of the authors listed above release a new book, I am definitely one of the first to get it. I would advise you to read from them all but start with the one holding the information you need **now**! Don't get caught up in titles and names, rather get caught up with information that is appropriate at the right time. Who has the information you need right now? Read and learn from them. It allows you to take information from experts and download it into your brain. It saves you years on your journey to success because they are the shortcut.

The power of reading allows you to take words written by others, convert them into ideas, and have your own experience. You begin to draw out the necessary blueprint for your vision. That is how you cut down decades of research and turn it into months or even days. So, it's time. It's time to take that book from shelf-help and turn it into self-help. Stop letting those books collect dust. Wipe them off and start reading. And please, do not speed read. It takes away from the experience. I personally prefer to read slowly so I can savor the moment and accurately digest the information. Taking my time allows me to take in what is being said and read with intention. Remember, I am an active reader. So, when I read, I always have these four things ready and handy: a pen, highlighter, sticky notes, and a bookmark. You should always have these items readily available or at least have a bookmark and highlighter. You can always go back and find a pen if one wasn't available at the moment.

Most importantly, get plugged in. Seek out masterminds, summits, conventions, webinars, seminars, mentors, programs, courses, bootcamps, retreats, podcasts, and YouTube channels that can lead you to the next big idea or business. Become a lifelong learner. It will keep you healthy, and happier and the more you know, the more you can earn. Stay reading, continue stimulating the mind.

That's the power of reading.

6
The Art of Journaling

Journaling is the activity of keeping a diary known as a journal. In this journal you are able to record things from your day-to-day events and memories you don't want to forget. Journaling is your thoughts placed on paper. Downloading what you are thinking into a safe place where no one can judge or question you because it's only for you. It's your own safe haven.

Journaling is personal. There is no "one-way fits all" method. No one can tell you how or when to journal. It's an activity you can either do in the morning to start your day or at midday to keep track of things that have already occurred. Or you can also journal during your evening routine to brain vomit all your thoughts and feelings.

The great Seneca once said, "When the light has been removed and my wife has fallen silent, aware of this habit that's now mine, I examine my entire day and go back over what I've done and said, hiding nothing from myself, passing nothing by." This is such a deep quote by Seneca because what he is saying is that he doesn't hide or keep anything from himself. Also stating journaling is where we can improve ourselves. We must be willing to confront ourselves daily with the reality of how we're living.

When we can see our mistakes on paper, we get a better view of how we can better ourselves. Improvement can only come when one is honest with their day-to-day actions. We must be real, authentic, and genuine at all times. You have all these thoughts inside you, but you can never put those thoughts to use until they're out of your head. Same goes with your full tank of gas, if you don't use your car, what's the point of having a full tank? We must be able to put our lives up for review to catch a greater insight into who we are.

Moreover, journaling helps to slow us down. It aids in bringing our racing minds from 80 miles per hour (MPH) to a steady 20 MPH, giving us an opportunity to learn new things about ourselves. Our minds are in a constant race by themselves all day. And if we don't stop to write down what we may need to do for the day or the week, we will fall into the "I forgot" mentality. It's important to write down upcoming appointments, needed groceries, etc. because as much as we want to remember, our minds are running at a high-level speed which will make us forget if we do not write things down.

Another reason why journaling is significant, the more we write on paper the less stressful our lives will be. Don't journal just to pass time. Become intentional and allow your thoughts to change you from good to great. And keep in mind the enemy of this world is great at being good. He's good at polluting one's mind with trauma, depression, and anxiety. The enemy of this world knows that if he wins our minds then he wins our day. But in journaling, your true feelings will be exposed, and you'll be able to see where you are and how you'll have to shift to get yourself back on track.

John Maxwell says, "Reflective thinking turns experience into insight." So it's not the actual experience you live that will teach you, but the reflection of that experience. The journaling process will help create these new insights which in turn helps you show up in life differently. Reflecting on an experience means sitting with yourself and writing down what has occurred, how it occurred, and what made it turn out the way that it did. Reflecting on an experience turns into insight giving us an opportunity to tap into our blind spots which allows us to see things from a different perspective. Let me add, perspective is powerful. No two people will see things the same. Perception is reality! You must become aware of the people you are learning from because the more you know about their successes and failures the more you'll be able to relate. Not all people who are famous for their fancy quotes or powerful sayings will just openly share their successes. I can share with you a list of amazing writers who have also shared the failures which they've written about in their own journals:

- John Adams
- Ralph Waldo
- Benjamin Franklin
- Marcus Aurelius
- Leonardo Da Vinci
- Thomas Edison
- Charles Darwin
- Mark Twain
- Elbert Einstein

The names listed above have left us with a great blueprint to follow despite the failures we may come across. Still, journaling is number one for mental stress release. By journaling and placing our thoughts on paper, we gain better control of our symptoms and mood behaviors. Below is a list of the additional benefits of journaling:

Benefits of Journaling:

- Reduces stress
- Inspires to achieve
- Boosts your mood
- Creates a rush of Red Bull inspiration
- Improves mental health
- Encourages self-confidence
- Boosts emotional intelligence
- Inspires creativity
- Enhances critical thinking skills
- Sharpens your memory
- Improves your writing skills
- Improves your communication skills
- Keeps thoughts organized

Putting things on paper helps to declutter the mind and brings self-awareness to those disorganized ideas we have in our minds. You'll be surprised how creative one becomes once the mind is released from its daily deep thoughts. Thoughts through journaling help in keeping track of any growth processes. This way, you can always go back to certain days, or even years, and reflect on how you've grown.

Being able to reflect on past writings can often contribute to the creation of the next course or program. With years and time in between, you should have mastered how to transition from one main point to another, utilizing that to help others unload what may be their emotional baggage. Never underestimate what you feel you may need to write down. What doesn't make sense to you now may later be the breakthrough for another person. Release it on paper.

Don't be that person who only journals the "good days." Don't be afraid to write about the bad days too. Those will be the days from which you will pull your strength. They serve a purpose as well. Looking over those bad days will allow you to show more gratitude for where you are now. It will become a form of therapy. Before you know it, journaling will be known for your morning gratitude and your evening reflections.

Think of journaling as your personal filing cabinet. Storing away documents, insights, breakthroughs, lessons learned, personal development, growth processes, wins, losses, ideas and so much more. There is no limit to what and how much you can release from your mind and store up in your journal. My time of journaling sometimes is organized and other times it's a brain dump. Dumping whatever is on my mind that is serving as either bad energy or sometimes creative and positive ideas. And if I can't find the words to write, I'm sure to write at least one line a day (worst case scenario).

There is actually a journal called, "One Line A Day," which serves as a five-year memory book. The goal is to write just one line for each day of the year allowing you to go back at the end of the year and recap your daily entries. Can you imagine having a book to reference the past five years of your life, where you've talked about all the cool stuff that has happened in your life? It will feel like going back in time and having a chat with history. It's also an easy way to gauge progress.

Journaling can be done for anything, not just good and bad days. For example, journaling can be used as your fitness accountability partner, using it to record and keep track of workouts and calorie intakes. Journaling your fitness progress also allows you to staple before and after pictures admitting you to see your overall goal be met week by week.

Maybe you want to use journaling to ask yourself questions, but you are not sure where to start. Here are a few journal-prompts to help you get started:

Journal Prompts

- What would I do if I could not fail?

- Do I have any regrets in life?
- What does my best "self" look like?
- Who can I count on?
- Who can count on me?
- Why am I not where I want to be?
- What are my business ideas?
- What makes me special and unique?
- What are my lingering fears?
- What do I worry about most?
- If I could do it all over again, what would I change?
- Advice for my future self.
- Where are some places I desire to go?
- How would a personalized daily prayer for myself sound like?
- How can I better listen to the voice inside of me?
- What would I want it to say on my headstone/tombstone?
- What does my last letter to my children sound like as they read it years from now?

Now it's time to journal. Before moving on to the next chapter, find a book, find a pen, and begin putting thoughts to paper. Robert Fulghum said it best, "The examined life is no picnic." Meaning that, when you begin to journal, you will notice the sunny good days, but you will also run across dark clouds that seem to shower you with endless rain. Keep in mind, those dark days are not who you are. It's just what's happening to you now. Learn to appreciate self-examination. It will provide you with a sense of understanding and motivation.

Now let's write!

7
Commonplacing

What is commonplacing? If you're anything like me, I once had my hand raised unsure of what this was either. However, I've come to learn that commonplacing is actually common among writers and poets. Commonplacing is simply the art of assembling together certain information for future reference. Not anything you may have to use now, right at this moment, but sources you may need to reference later.

Another example is sorting or filing specific quotes, notes, stats, and ideas from books, mentors, YouTube, magazines, seminars, etc. There's nothing extravagant about the practice itself outside of having a name that seems unfamiliar and too complicated to understand without research on it; commonplacing. Yet, unknowingly, we commonplace on a daily basis especially if you're into Pinterest. Pinterest is one location where people all over the world come to share their scrapbooks. Pinterest allows you to save and file away your "favorites" until it is needed.

Now, let's not be confused with a journal versus a commonplace book. A journal is more of a day-to-day memory of events that have occurred and a process for ideation. Whereas a commonplace book is based on existing sources needed for use at a later point in time. More successful people use commonplace books to store the wisdom and knowledge that they've learned throughout their years dating back to the 14th century.

Ryan Holiday is someone I would highly recommend you follow if you're not already. He's an author from Texas with an amazing bookstore. He's also learned the meaning of commonplacing from his mentor Robert Greene. Holiday adds to his commonplace book quotes that have stuck out to him from other authors or articles. Even if it's a one-liner that's good enough for him. He jots it down to have it around for later reference, even to use in his own writings, or simply to inspire someone else.

As for myself, I have a huge filing system in place right in my home. In my commonplace area, I have over 150 categories stored with topics such as faith, motivation, growth, mindset, failure, success, finance, team building, and so much more. My method of commonplacing may seem taxing to some but here are my steps. As I'm reading a book, if I come across a quote, a saying, or anything I know I can and will reference later, I jot it down. Then, I take an index card, I write down the page number and book where the thought came from, I write the quote or saying while also giving it a label so I can store it properly in the right section.

Next, the card gets placed in my filing cabinet which is my commonplace area. It's safely stored and when I need to use it, I'll know right where to look to get it. This method takes a lot more discipline and motivation than just taking notes and filing them away without labeling them. When I am asked to speak on leadership, I go to my filing cabinet, I pull out my index cards under the topic "leadership" and I start the draft of my speech using my index cards. This makes speaking come a bit easier when you have strong notes and quotes to glean from.

Steven Johnson said it best as I quote him, "Commonplacing is transcribing interesting or inspirational passages from one's reading, assembling a *personalized* encyclopedia of quotation." Meaning, it has to become personal. You have to pull from books, magazines, articles, and newspapers information that can and will be beneficial in the long run. This is not an activity done such as coloring a book and staying in the lines just to have a pretty picture.

The art of commonplacing has to mean more than a picture shown.

Notes taken and stored have to be taken seriously, in order to use when called for training, seminars, or even as a guest on a podcast show. It reminds me of the six P's: Proper Prior Planning Prevents Poor Performance. This is why during my evening routine, I commonplace all of the index cards that I may have created throughout the day. I won't end my evening routine until all cards are put away because remember, what you don't complete the night before you add to your morning routine.

A couple of notable people who have utilized commonplacing successfully are as follows:
- Marcus Aurelius
- Erasmus
- John Locke
- Thomas Jefferson
- E.M Forster
- Steven Johnson

- Ronald Reagan
- Ryan Holiday
- John Maxwell
- Mark Twain
- David Rockefeller
- Napoleon Bonaparte

While there are so many I can speak of, I'll narrow it down to Steven Johnson. He is currently the author of more than 10 books with the book titled, *Everything Bad is Good for you: How Today's Popular Culture Is Actually Making Us Smarter* released in 2005 and known as a best-seller. When Steven was asked how he was able to write informative, golden nugget books, he mentioned it was through commonplacing. Every one of his books is filled with meat on the bone. Steven has created his own commonplacing method. Once he recorded random notes every day and over time, he accumulated over 100,000 words on his Google docs. From those notes, he was able to write and publish books that were beneficial to those who chose to read them.

To think how one can accumulate over 100,000 words to store and put away requires much attention to detail. Commonplacing can be very time consuming and at times feel tedious. Rest assured, it's so worth it. Especially if you are a coach, author, speaker, manager, trainer, or writer of any kind.

Here's why I press the issue of continuous growth in knowledge. It's been said throughout the years that knowledge is the accumulation of information while wisdom is knowing how to apply it (Unknown). While knowledge is necessary for growth, wisdom plays an even more important factor in the matter because as I mentioned before, it's not what you know, it's what you do with what you know. Head knowledge is not enough. Knowledge says to jot this down or make note of this, but wisdom says to store it, label it, and put it up for later because wisdom is the application of having and showing common sense. And what better place to store common sense than in a commonplace book?

Words and quotes can be taken and stored from just about anywhere; from a conversation with your mentor, someone with whom you had a virtual coffee, a co-worker, or a video or show you watched. The people and places you get information from to store in your commonplace book are endless. Always be on the lookout for new content to store away.

Vital points and phrases can also be found on your drive home as you listen to motivational speakers and podcasts. I like to call this your university on wheels. We have the necessary tools and devices to learn right at our fingertips. YouTube will tell you everything you need to know in just about any category. So, there are no excuses for our thought level and growth to be taken to the next level.

Robert Greene, an influencer and bestselling author, reads about 250 books a year. He creates note cards for each book he reads. It's been said that if the book he's reading is good enough, he'll walk away with about 30-40 note cards. If not so great, he'll walk away with about 10-15. Greene even color coordinates his note cards and loads the margins of each book with comments, remarks, and his two cents.

I want to share an important statement that was made by Douglas Brinkley. On behalf of former President Ronald Reagan, Reagan was asked, if his home was to burn down and he would lose it all but could save one item, what item would that be? Douglas states the former President's response was, "He would save his commonplace book." That says a lot about the information that's been saved, jotted down, and stored for future reference. I'm no President of the United States but I can relate to the importance of a former President's commonplace book because my life was highly impacted in a positive way through my own commonplacing.

I started my journey with commonplacing back in 2019, around the same time I decided to read more. And it has shifted my life for the better. I can only imagine how much further along I would have been had I started a lot sooner. Commonplacing has created more opportunities for me because when I was called for an assignment, I was ready. I would go into my filing cabinet, search through my index cards, and prepare a message that would bless the house on any occasion. If you were to ask me which necessary tools are needed to start today, I would say:

- Visit Staples or Amazon
- 3x5 or 4x6 index cards
- Storage container (shoe box or some kind of filing cabinet)
- A pen with a fine tip

- Color dividers for the index cards

I'll leave you with this summarized message from Admiral William H. McRaven-United States Navy Seal Team

*Nothing matters but your will to succeed.
It all starts with how you get up in the morning,
and how you make your bed.
You'll never do the big things right if you
can't do the little things right.
You can always measure a person by the
size of their heart. You will fail often
but never give up. The next generation
will live in a world better than we are in today if
we do not give up. We must complete each
task given to us. We must not be afraid
of the sharks that we'll come in contact with
in this world. We must fight on.
We must carry the power of hope.
We are the power of one.*

This speech is not given in the order in which Admiral stated. It was simply shared here to give you a sense of hope, to not give up but to continue on for your best is waiting on the other side.

8
Examination of Conscience

What is an examination of conscience? It is the process of examining past thoughts, deeds, and actions made towards people, self, and God. It's a state of looking inwardly at our hearts and souls and seeing how we've hurt those we say we love and how we have hurt God.

When you are examining your conscience, you must be honest, straightforward, and willing to tell the truth even if it reveals some ugly truths concerning self. Deep questions you must ask, one in particular, which I tend to suggest is whose flag do you carry? Do you stand to carry the flag that represents God and His love and faithfulness or the flag of the enemy (Satan, the devil), which causes more destruction than good? Whose flag do you carry on a daily basis?

Daily acts of examining my own conscience take place more so during my evening routine. This helps me take a deeper look at how I behaved that day and who I may have been turned off by, unveiling a deeper level of who I am and asking myself if my actions today were in line with who I am called to be, who I want to be, and who I need to become.

All three (who, want, need), play a significant part when taking self to the next level. As a Catholic, I am aware that examining my conscience will be a daily battle. And not just for me, but for you too when you've chosen to follow good over evil. It doesn't matter what your faith is, I still urge you to examine your conscience every night. We all have one whether you are Christian or not. When you decide to align your life with the things of God, be advised much time will be needed for growth to show up, for improvement to be seen, and for the map of our lives to be navigated with a better and clearer conscience. It will be uphill all the way but so worth it.

They say with age comes wisdom, but I tend to think that's not completely true. I like to think that sometimes age comes alone. Wisdom is not attached to age and maturity certainly isn't. I know some grown boys that haven't hit the corner to becoming men. Wisdom is not given to the "aged" but to those that can understand at any age that we are but of the dust of this world and, without the grace and mercy of God, we are absolutely nothing.

You must examine your conscience to gain a better perspective and know what must be done in order to be better. When one can deepen their connection with faith and its core values, it not only helps to respond more efficiently but also promotes better learning while gaining a greater understanding of self. Examining the conscience is seeing the greater picture, and shaping better relationships, whether with family, friends, your spouse, or your children. Having a greater perspective of self is the common denominator of less stress and anxiety.

Before 2019, I wasn't making the time to better myself while staying connected as a husband to my wife and a father to my children. The only picture I had in mind was what was happening then at the moment. Seeing how that was not working for me and my family I began to shift my thinking leading into 2019 (my changing year) I began to ask myself more penetrating questions. Is this how I truly want to live the rest of my life? Having 24 hours in the day but only a five-minute conversation with my wife in passing and not much of a dialogue with my kids? NO! This can't be my life.

We were not going to become the next statistic of couples that end in divorce because of lack of communication. So, I examined myself. I examined my own conscience, and built enough courage to say out loud, "I will change." From that moment forward in 2019, I made the commitment to spend more time with my wife and children. We were no longer the couple that sat on the couch for two hours and only spoke for two minutes. No more were we numbing our brains in the same room, instead we shifted together, examining together what needed to be different and worked accordingly.

A Greek philosopher named Socrates once said, "The unexamined life is not worth living." Socrates was not suggesting for anyone to end their life through death, rather he was stating that any human that withdraws themselves from their purpose of life has now cheated themselves from living out their full potential. And I would add, it is best for us to live out our purpose because, while there are millions of us (humans) across the globe, we each hold a special DNA that can unlock certain things happening in this world. Make your life worth living.

There may be some of you who feel like there are endless decisions that must be made on any given day. First slow down, as I stated in a previous chapter, and learn how to take your mind from running 80 MPH to a steady 20 MPH. Sometimes we need to slow down to speed up. Examine the conscience. Decide what is most important to accomplish first and start there. The desire to become better does not necessarily mean to do more of multiple things but it means to do more of the same thing so you can better yourself in that task or area. Becoming better means becoming intentional.

Let's go deeper. Examining the conscience is not only for self versus others. It's also self versus God. The question one must ask here is, "Have I considered God my Father? Did I offer Him my work today? Have I neglected the children that He has blessed me with? Have I neglected the spouse He's blessed me with? Have I made great use of my time with Him today?" To insure I start my day off on the right track I begin with these four things:

- Prayer
- Silent Meditation
- Placing myself in the presence of God
- Acknowledging His response to me

I start with prayer because it's how I connect with God on a deep level. Conversation that builds my relationship with Him. Prayer allows me to express my gratitude to Him. It creates a sense of awareness on how I'm living. I also ask for forgiveness in the areas where I fell short. I include others I need to pray for and, of course, ask for certain things near and dear to my heart understanding it's ultimately God's will that will be done.

Then, I meditate. I sit in silence concentrating on my breathing and working on clearing my mind so I may hear what He has to say. During my meditation, I ponder on His goodness. If my mind begins to drift and wander, I'm kind to myself. I pivot, bringing back my focus to the main thing. I sit in meditation until my mind is clear enough to sit in His presence.

Next, when my mind is clear of all distractions, I place myself in the presence of God. Still not saying a word just posturing myself in His presence. Preparing to hear what He may say to me when He speaks. I've learned that when sitting in the presence of God, it's always best to be quiet. If He's speaking and you're trying to also get a word in, you'll be sure to miss what He has to say. And because He is such a loving God, if you missed what He said the first time, He'll bring it back around one more time in one way or another.

Lastly, I acknowledge His response to me by how I act after my time in prayer. I examine my thoughts throughout the day. I examine my actions. I examine my deeds done to others. I examine my conscience midday just to ensure I am still in alignment with my assignment. Most of all, I pause and ask, "What could I have done better today thus far?" And I allow the truth of that answer to lead me through the rest of my day.

Here are a few things that you can consider in order to help you examine your conscience:

- Schedule your daily reflections
- Start with five minutes and increase your time gradually
- Challenge yourself with difficult questions and be honest
- Take insights from your personal journal entries and see where and how you can shift to better thinking
- Adjust immediately and without delay
- Embrace the journey

One vital factor you must consider is, if your behavior is not aligned with what you believe, then ask yourself if you really believe. That can be a bitter pill to swallow for sure. Do you believe in your own vision when your actions are contrary to what you've set out to accomplish? Be willing to make it a habit to check in with yourself to see where you really are in life. Not just for your own agenda but for God's will for your life.

Examining the conscience goes hand in hand with giving yourself a hard reality check, seeing if where you are now is leading you to where you want to be. Are you behaving in a way with how you see yourself two years from now, five years from now, or even ten years from now? When we are honest with ourselves, we'll be able to see ourselves when we get off course. When we do, we must recommit ourselves to getting back on track. We must constantly course correct along the journey. Practicing self-reflection will require much discipline and a lot of time with *SELF*.

In order for you to have time with yourself, you must hit the pause button of your life. Slowing down the pace even taking the next exit ramp and taking no one with you. It's an exit only for one - YOU. There will be times when the examination of conscience will advise you to slow down in order to speed back up again. When you slow down the pace of your life, you'll be able to see things on a ground level.

Aristotle once said, "Knowing yourself is the beginning of all wisdom." Meaning no deceit, falseness, dishonestly, or unfair action will be a part of your daily habit. When you can come to grips with your true self, what needs to happen in your life will have its place. Adapting, strategizing, and planning for success will come as second nature. And failure will never be looked upon as a dead end but as a new beginning.

In closing, the examination of conscience for the believer is tied with and to the Holy Spirit. Allowing us to depend on His guidance and become receptive to His will. This gives us the chance to question ourselves to assure we are in the correct standing for self-growth. Asking questions such as:

- What have I done wrong?
- What have I done right?
- What could I have done better?
- Did I offer up my work to God today?
- Did I neglect my duties as a spouse?
- Did I neglect my duties as a parent?
- Did I make good use of my time?
- Did I pray today with focus and attention?
- Did I criticize anyone?
- Have I remained humble?
- Was I forgiving?
- Did I pray for others?
- Was I prideful or arrogant?
- Was I envious or judgmental?

- Am I stuck in fear and not taking action on something that must be done?
- Is there something or someone I need to get right with?
- Was I charitable today?
- Did I give in to procrastination on something important?
- How did I express my gratitude today?

I leave you with those few questions to stir the soul and lead you to examine your conscience.

9
Personal Project Time

Personal project time is a title I gave myself to acknowledge working on something that will move the needle in my life, business, and career to a higher and more successful level. You must work on your own hustle apart from your everyday job. Too often, too many people are working jobs they absolutely hate, clocking in wishing they were clocking out. Their job doesn't pay enough, but they keep this cycle; why?

Most Americans are caught up in the "rat race." This race is tiring and competitive and usually is the cause of having to work two jobs versus one. The rat race is working hours upon hours just to purchase senseless things; expensive jewelry, cars, houses, etc. So many people chase "fast money," hoping something will change. But how many of you know that *hope* is not a plan?

Hope is a feeling that something good will come out of what you're working on. What that "something" is may be unclear, as hope is only a feeling without a strategy. Desire takes that same hope and puts it to work. Desire says I have made up my mind, and I will see this project out until it is complete. Nothing and no one can stop the man or woman who desires to succeed and has a made-up mind. Hope just wishes, but Proverbs 13:12 says, "Hope deferred makes the heart sick: but when the desire comes, it is a tree of life." Meaning that hope when it is put off or delayed can build frustrations and cause sickness in the body. But when desire shows up, it brings into reality a foundation for the hope one had. Desire brings forth the fruit needed for the personal project to come to fruition. And the fulfillment of it will be as a tree of life, plentiful and vibrant.

You must have and show a plan to change your present life. Change is rewarding, whether you start with two or three side hustles, change is rewarding. The multimillionaire, coach and bestselling author, Dan Lok had once been in debt up to his neck. He'd gone from in debt to trash man to a multimillionaire with an estimated net worth of over $81 million dollars. He gives the four stages of life:

- Survivor
- Security
- Success
- Significance

The first stage of life is "survivor," which consists of living paycheck to paycheck. Paying the bills and caring for yourself while having more month than money. Survivor places you in the position of robbing Peter to pay Paul, just trying to get by. Before you know it, you're drained.

After the first stage comes stage 2, security. This place in life gives you more breathing room. You're not in survivor mode any longer; you've improved a little more in life. You no longer have to bum a couch at a friend's house; you don't need four roommates to help pay rent. At this point in life, it's just you and possibly your small family with your spouse and children. You're eating better, but the downfall is that people typically get comfortable here and stay. They never move on from this stage. Generally because there is a sense of basic security and comfort and less risk to try for more. It's so easy to stay in your comfort zone and live a very predictable life that doesn't require much. But when you do decide to move on, trust that the next move is to success – the third stage.

With success, you now have everything you need, want, and can imagine, whether it's the mansion or the house by the lake. You're successful and doing well for yourself. You have the cars of your dreams and can travel worldwide. People now begin to look up to you. You're a leader, you've changed your life, and now you're at the place of success with the top 3%. But even at this stage, it's easy to become driven by the materialistic things you can now afford, so much so you lose sight of your vision. Believe it or not, the stage of success is not your arrival, you can't just have success for the sake of having it. It doesn't and cannot stop here. There's one more stage to climb, significance.

Significance has a new mindset, one that focuses on the meaning of all that has been obtained. Life and money mean something totally different when you're at this stage than they did in the first three stages. In the significance stage, you begin to think about the legacy left behind once you close your eyes to life. Significance says, "Alright, I'm successful. I have the house, cars, family, food, and money, but what's next? Who can I teach, and who can I leave an impact on? Is there anybody that is better off in this world because I was here?

Every one of us has to journey through these four stages of life. It's just a matter of time. To have money without impact is just like living paycheck to paycheck and still being broke before you get the check. Getting to your significance stage, you must ask yourself, "How much impact did I create in this life? Don't become so successful that your point of existence no longer matters. Continue to serve, continue to help, continue to build, and continue bringing someone up the ladder of success with you.

If you're a new entrepreneur who's just starting off, do not bypass stage one to get to the stage of significance. Dan Lok once stated, "If you miss a step, you miss people you were supposed to impact." At every stage of your life, you will come across individuals placed in your path for a reason. Don't become so desperate for success that you fail purposefully. Don't live paycheck to paycheck (stage one) yet assume to portray stage four.

I am personally at a place in life where I can help and serve in a major way. But I am still after significance! Did I start here? No. As you might recall reading in the beginning. Just like everyone else, I, too, started my journey going through stage one, survivor. I paused my life to take a look at a clock. I realized that there were only 24 hours in a day. Eight hours to work, eight hours to sleep, and eight hours to make my dreams a reality. I realized I needed more time, so I began to pull from other areas. I began to say; I don't really need eight hours of sleep. Six hours would do me just fine. So, I took the two remaining hours left over from the category of "sleep," and I moved them to my "hours for self." Now giving myself 10 hours a day to work for me.

If we are honest, we all have time for personal project time. Think about it, some of you clock into an eight-hour shift, but how many are actually physically working for eight straight hours? Not many. Some take extended breaks, and that last hour of work, you can pretty much forget it. Your day is basically over, you're just waiting now to clock out. But what are you doing in between times? How are you building for true success? What book(s) are you reading during those lunch breaks? What are you feeding yourself that will benefit you in the long run? It's been said once, and I'll say it twice, "People make time for what they want." Do you know what you desire today and not just hoping for?

If you're like most people desiring financial freedom, one thing I recommend during your personal project time is to develop a high-income skill. A high-income skill allows you to earn $10,000 a month or more. How? By providing a service, people need and don't know how to do or accomplish on their own. It's called specialized knowledge. Trust me, people will pay a lot of money for specialized knowledge. Gain a skill that no one will be able to take from you, but the service is transferable from industry to industry.

Here are a few examples of businesses that can lead you to make six figures a year:

- Copywriter
- Creative Writer
- Consultant
- Digital Marketer
- Content Creator
- Public Speaking
- Translator
- Photographer
- Programmer
- High Ticket Closer
- Speaker
- Coach

The way to advance in life and grow in your personal development is to tackle one project at a time. Become a master and utilize it in other areas. Take the example of a copywriter. One might start off by getting certified, then becoming a consultant, teaching others how to become copywriters. By mastering one skill, you've developed two incomes. With knowledge and enough experience, you can become a high-income earner. Learn to stack high-income skills. That's where the money starts to get exciting.

I've been determined since 2019 to put out the effort needed to become successful. The momentum has been amazing. In the last 12 months alone I have achieved a few things of which I am most proud:

- Launched a successful subscription based global network
- Launched a high-ticket program in high-performance coaching
- Earned my John Maxwell Certification
- Became a successful speaker, coach, and trainer
- Launched my own merchandise line of branded products
- Became a five-time bestselling author
- Launched multiple LIVE events for entrepreneurs

I am proud of what I have been able to accomplish in such a short period of time. I leave you with these last encouraging words; go out and work. Be patient with your process, for not all processes will move at the same speed. Once you target your high-income skill, become the master in the field. Some months may land you $5K, or even $10K. If you remain consistent enough, you'll eventually hit your bigger goals and start living that life of significance before you know it.

Start the process.
Develop the side hustle.
If you enjoy your day job,
stay there, that's fine.

But if

YOU

want more than a
9-5, start today with your
PPT (personal project time).

Closing

In closing, I hope that this book has truly inspired you to step into your calling to really become that person you aspire to be. I hope you're inspired to genuinely elevate your life like never before. I am confident that you now have some tools to help take your life personally and professionally to the next level. Keep in mind that there will be times when you will catch yourself along the journey of success with self doubt and becoming fearful of the unknown, but I want to leave you with this, do it anyway. Do it when you're afraid. Do it when you're uncertain of the outcome. Do it when you have to stand alone. Do it when no one is clapping for you. Do it anyway. If you need to doubt anything, doubt your doubts!

The truth is we all have seeds of greatness in us because of our Creator. We are capable of accomplishing anything we set our minds to do. I am a prime example of what you get when you tap into your potential. And I am barely scratching the surface. Trust me, it's been a tough journey. Even so, it's nothing you cannot create for yourself too.

While writing this book, I have successfully been scaling two businesses to multiple six figures each with a family of seven and holding a day job too. The Morning and Evening Routine Mastery Program (under my company The Entrepreneur's Bookshelf) and the Connected Leaders Academy have been taking off. I've made investments in the tens of thousands of dollars in myself over time, but I always saw the bigger picture. I knew my investments would pay off eventually, and I am seeing the fruits of my labor now. My life, my family's life, and those who come in contact with me, their lives will never be the same.

In just a short period of time, I have been able to make over $180,000 with my bestselling program, "The Morning & Evening Routine Mastery." This has happened in under a year. The Connected Leaders Academy started out as just an idea and now has become a six-figure business. As Napoleon Hill repeats in his book, "Think and Grow Rich," it all starts with an idea.

From the day I thought of the idea of the Connected Leaders Academy, it took me two weeks to create a logo, name, and price point. The more I thought about it and envisioned it, the more the business began to unveil itself to me. I activated a ten-plus benefit package for the members; I ran with it and didn't look back. There was no delay and I simply executed. Sometimes the success we seek lies in simply taking action.

Today I stand with one community, one tribe, one family. The vision is to have 1,000 members by the end of 2023. Stay tuned; pay attention. The grand vision is to have the CLA Tribe reach global impact in over 100 countries with millions of members. The dream is very much alive, and the vision is massive. The launching of this book is truly a dream come true in itself. This book will serve many and live on beyond my years. What a legacy to leave behind.

In addition to launching two multiple 6-figure businesses, I also became a Maxwell certified coach, trainer and speaker, got into the LIVE events space, launched a merchandise line of branded products, became a 5-time bestselling author, among other projects all in under one year. I now have 8 income streams. I wholeheartedly believe there is nothing I cannot do. I do not allow mental procrastination to take over or get in the way of what I desire to accomplish. I want that for YOU today!

Your time to start is now. If I can build two companies in seven months and scale them to six-figure businesses, among all the other moving parts, I know it can be done and you can do something similar or more. The only thing stopping you from your next level is you. I assure you there is more within reach for you right now. How big are you thinking? What's the next event you can tap into?

As a matter of fact, my first large scale event is just around the corner from the publishing of this book. October 13th through the 15th of 2023, in Maryland, I will have entrepreneurs from all parts of the country attend. It will be our first annual CLA Global Summit. I am expecting to have 1,000 entrepreneurs in the room from all over the world and across the USA. While it is no easy task to pull off a summit this size, there's no turning back. I have signed on the dotted line. I have given it my "yes" and I am committed to seeing it come to life. This summit has been the biggest contract I've ever signed, and it feels good. This is the life of an entrepreneur. Playing full out!

If you're reading this book, it's because you are an entrepreneur or an inspiring entrepreneur, and ready for change. Let me say this, don't be afraid of failure, and don't be afraid of success. I didn't allow either one to stop me. My encouragement here is not to impress you but to express the importance of believing in yourself, taking action, and being fully committed to what you set out to do. Believe in yourself and know who you are. Walk in your full potential. Your time is now. Forget about the past. The future is not here yet. What you have now is YOUR moment.

What you want to achieve will not come easy. It takes hard work, discipline, consistency, and daily commitment. Make no excuses. Mark my words. There is nothing special about me or anything golden that was given to me. I had no special treatment of any kind. I simply got tired of being average and believed my family deserved more from me. I knew I was not tapping into who I was called to be. With that, I made a commitment to change.

We only get one life. Let this book serve not just to motivate you and make you feel good but to give you ideas for strategies to apply today to your life and everyday business. By doing so, I pray you begin to see the needle moving toward success.

Start today.

Start now.

Don't look back.

And stay with me as I take my businesses to multimillionaire status.

HERE IS THE KICKER...

I want to HELP you do the same! Connect with me TODAY! I would love to share with you how The Morning & Evening Routine Mastery Program can take your personal and professional life to NEW HEIGHTS. This book is just the tip of the iceberg of The Morning & Evening Routine Mastery. I have helped tons of people change their lives and make drastic changes for the better in just 8 weeks. If you are serious about leveling up across the board, this program is for you. I want to coach you and hold you accountable along the way.

https://linktr.ee/jaesco25